SUMMARY

Dr. Gundry's
Diet Evolution

Book by
Steven Gundry

Turn Off the Genes That
Are Killing You and Your Waistline

Rapid-Summary

© Copyright 2018 - Present.
All rights reserved.

This document is geared towards providing reliable information in regards to the topic and issue covered. The publication is sold with the idea that the publisher is not required to render accounting, officially permitted, or otherwise, qualified services. If advice is necessary, legal, or professional, a practiced individual in the profession shall be ordered.

- From a Declaration of Principles which was accepted and approved equally by a Committee of the American Bar Association and a Committee of Publishers and Associations.

In no way is it legal to reproduce, duplicate, or transmit any part of this document in either electronic means or in printed format. Recording of this publication is strictly prohibited and any storage of this document is not allowed unless with written permission from the publisher. All rights reserved.

The information provided herein is stated to be truthful and consistent, in that any liability, in terms of inattention or otherwise, by any usage or abuse of any policies, processes, or directions contained within is solely and completely the responsibility of the recipient reader. Under no circumstances will any legal responsibility or blame be held against the publisher for any reparation, damages, or monetary loss due to the information herein, either directly or indirectly.

Respective authors own all copyrights not held by the publisher.

Before we proceed...

Feel free to follow us on social media to be notified of future summaries.

1- Facebook: BookSummaries

   https://www.facebook.com/BookSummaries-1060732983986564/

2- Instagram: BookSummaries

   https://www.instagram.com/booksummaries/

Table of Contents

Introduction 1

Chapter 1: Your Genes are running the Show 3

Chapter 2: We Are What We Eat 7

Chapter 3: The Diet at a Glance 9

Chapter 4: The First Two Weeks 15

Chapter 5: What's Off the Menu? 19

Chapter 6: The Teardown Continues 23

Chapter 7: Settling In 29

Chapter 8: Begin the Restoration 33

Chapter 9: Picking up the Pace 37

Chapter 10: Thriving for a Good, Long Time 41

Chapter 11: Tricking Your Genes: Beyond Diet 43

Quiz and Answers 47

Conclusion 51

Introduction

This book discusses the Diet Evolution, which consists of three phases. What's great about this diet plan is that it teaches you a new routine and habit along with exercise. It is not just a diet but a way of life. The diet evolution aims to hinder the "killer genes" from activating so that you will have a long and healthy life. Also, after three months into the program, you will have a new set of healthy cells. It's like being an entirely different person.

Phase 1 or the Teardown phase encourages you to lose weight by increasing the intake of greens and opting for meat that comes from plant-eating animals only. Animals that eat plants act as mediators so that you can gain plant nutrients and proteins.

Phase 2 or the Restoration phase requires that you eliminate the mediator and concentrate on the greens. It's like turning vegan. You are also recommended to take supplements to compensate for the other nutrients and to gain muscle mass. Nuts, salads, and smoothies are your main foods.

In phase 2 is where you also need to exercise. Either you go long distances in a slow and steady motion, or you go for short distances and sprint quickly. He also recommends a few minutes of strength training to increase muscle mass and tone them.

Dr. Gundry's Diet Evolution

The longevity phase or phase three is not for everyone. This is because most of the foods you eat will be raw. This is how your ancestors ate their food and is the secret to long life. Not a lot of people like eating raw foods so this may not be for you.

For people who are hesitant and don't know where to start, there is a meal plan and some recipes suited for the phase that you are in. You don't have to worry about what to eat. Another thing is that the menu in phase 1 can be recycled in phase 2 with slight changes. This means that you don't have to adjust again to the new food. Your eating habits will remain, and you'll get used to it.

Most of the diet evolution "Club members" were former patients who decided to change their lifestyle. Word-of-mouth is a successful method of advertising this diet plan. More people approach very eager to try this diet strategy mainly due to its successes. There were insulin-resistant patients who've had to deal with obesity for so long. There were also surgery patients with hip replacements due to obesity.

In this diet evolution, you are motivated to become a new person inside and out. Your lifestyle will change, and you will become healthier, good-looking, and feel good about it. Diet Evolution certainly aims to make people healthier and live longer.

Chapter 1:
Your Genes are running the Show

It's often said: "Back to Basics", and in this case, genes are the basics. Before interrogating your diet, you need to have the right knowledge about your genes and the role they play in your diet, health, and overall well-being. Many of us know that the genes we get from our parents are responsible for how we look, how we talk, specific attitudes, etc. but we remain ignorant concerning the roles they play in so many other areas of our lives. As absurd or unbelievable as it may sound, our genes deceive us into eating the wrong things and damaging our health. It's good for them but bad for us. Weird, right?

The relationship between our genes and our bodies can be likened to how a computer operating system is basically the force behind that computer. Our genes- activated or deactivated by food substances- hold information that instructs each cell on what to do at every point in time. Our genes are housed inside our bodies, and without their direction, we do not function, much like the computer and its operating system. As our bodies evolve, so do our genes, as this is necessary for their survival, and that is really all what the genes look out for.

It might seem quite defeating but the truth is that, much of what we do, say think, feel, how we age, etc. are controlled by something fundamentally beyond our control. If you're in doubt, decide right now to hold your breath and see for how long that lasts. Eventually, you're forced to resume breathing. This is because you not breathing does no good for your genes, so they disapprove of your actions and do not allow it. Basically, our bodies are on auto-pilot, controlled by specific gene-carrying cells. When we do the expected things- like breathing- everything goes on smoothly. But when we veer off and decide not to breathe for instance, we can get hurt.

Your genes are concerned about preservation, for themselves. They could care less about you, really. So they point you in three major directions, which are ultimately aimed at reproduction. When you reproduce, they are transferred and preserved.

- They drive you to get as much energy- in form of calories- with as little exertion as possible. The implication of this is glaring: excess calories + minimal activity = too much weight or obesity. Interestingly, your genes shut down when they detect you're getting more than you should. That's why obesity kills.

- They drive us to stay away and run from pain

- They drive us to seek pleasure- mating rituals, sexual intimacy, and other pleasure-inducing substances like addictive drugs and the world's commonest vice today, Sugar.

So basically, they want you to reproduce and preserve copies of your own genes, and they also want you not to waste too much time hanging around; in their opinion, it's not ideal that

Chapter 1: Your Genes are running the Show

you struggle for resources with younger ones. According to your genes, the more pleasurable (high-calorie) foods you eat, the higher your chances at surviving long enough to reproduce. And as you grow older, and your genes register this, your body will begin to deteriorate, telling you how you cannot continue to eat as much as the young ones.

Our genes are so intentional about their rules that whenever they detect threatening situations, they activate programmed responses to address the threats. You may not know, but there are more miscarriages of male unborn babies than female during food shortages. It's simple. Females are the ones designed to reproduce, so the more females, the more offspring, and continued preservation of genes. This is quite incredible, but this is how our genes work. Similarly, when you're the one threatening those rules, they take action, initiating what is called Killer Genes. They are so called because their job is to take out anyone they detect is competing unduly for scarce resources. They are a fundamental component in the human process of aging and death. So for instance, if you keep piling on the calories and are not keeping active enough, you become overweight, and the killer genes are alerted. Much the same way, when human activity decreases as a result of age advancement, the genes interpret it as you consuming useful resources when you can do little or nothing to contribute to the ecosystem. Over-stretching your body with rigorous exercise as well as smoking are also behaviors which trigger specific reactions and these reactions signal to your genes that you're not fit for existence. They- killer genes- inevitably swing into action.

Chapter 2:
We Are What We Eat

Have you noticed that more than 30 years ago people were slim? This is because they hadn't been introduced to the present Western diet. Looking at a fully clothed person, you could tell the condition of the body's vital organs. Having a large waistline is one of the signals that the killer genes have been activated.

Operating on people who had heart problems and obesity created the realization that all the research about nutrition was becoming useless. It is time to come up with a plan and stop this from happening. It is time to look at a new way of eating.

You will also notice the relationship of primates with fruits and that man is like an ape. Primates fatten up by eating fruits, especially during certain seasons. The main difference between herbivores and carnivores is that herbivores get all the proteins from plants and are 100% muscle. Both need calories – which are the energy count in food – and move around to obtain them.

The difference is that flesh-eaters (carnivores) consume more food but don't exert too much effort to secure it. Also, they tend to sleep it off. Herbivores, such as gorillas, pull off a few leaves or branches and exert energy. To maintain the supposed balance, carnivores eat herbivores so they can get plant nutrients. In addition, meat eaters need a higher metabolic rate to digest the food. Therefore, to save their metabolism, they need to sleep.

Your ancestors turned to meat for diet, and eating meat was due to the changes happening around them. Man's diet also evolved along with the social, climatic, and food-source changes that occurred over time. For example, if people lived near the lake, there was an abundance of fish. Why look for fruits and vegetables in the plains when they have easier access to the food sources in the water?

At the same time, if you live in a place where meat is abundant, why would you settle for hard-to-obtain veggies? Meat is also known to keep our body warmer, so when the climate changes, the diet also evolves. Man's diet evolves due to what is abundant now. Again, survival is the goal.

The Agricultural Revolution also brought about great changes to the human diet. It is much easier to milk a cow, kill a pig, and pick chicken eggs than harvest crops. Agriculture meant higher energy expenditures since machines were still not popular during that time. As time went by, it became easier to have access to meat than plant food. It is easier to just buy processed food or meat than planting your own leafy greens.

You will also notice why animals are not obese. Their genetic make-up, habitat, and exposure to sunlight contribute to the halt in the aging process and obesity. Likewise, their lifestyle is also a plus.

Chapter 3:
The Diet at a Glance

In this chapter, you will learn about the three food groups that are different from what we grew up with. They are categorized as "Friendly Foods," "Unfriendly Foods," and "Foods to Banish Initially."

"Friendly Foods" are protein-rich foods. These are mainly meat from grass-fed animals with no fat (e.g., lamb or venison), free-range poultry (e.g., duck or turkey), wild fish (e.g., Alaskan halibut or anchovies), and dairy products such as cheese, milk, and yogurt.

"Unfriendly foods" are foods that contain starch and turn to sugar when cooked. Examples are beets, carrots, corn, peas, and root vegetables such as turnips, sweet potatoes, winter squash, and yams. White foods are also to be avoided. These include anything sweet such as sugar and artificial sweeteners. Remember, when it's sweet, retreat!

Other white foods that are considered unfriendly are skim or fat-free milk, pasta, ranch dressing, white bread, frozen yogurt, mayonnaise, and ice cream. Also, there's "If it's beige, behave." These are bagels, coffee, cereals, chips, cookies, crackers, deep-fried food, low-fat processed food, pizza, and rolls.

Dr. Gundry's Diet Evolution

There are also the "killer fruits" that are loaded with sugar. These are dates, dried fruits, papayas, bananas, raisins. Alcohol is a no-no, as well as soda. Vegetable and fruit juices should also be removed from your diet.

There are foods that are to be "banished initially," meaning they slow down the weight-loss process so you need to abstain from them during the initial stages. These include brown food such as barley, brown rice, corn kernels, legumes, oats, and quinoa.

Also, it is recommended that you take supplements because they are a means of killing the sugar cravings. Here are some of the recommendations:

Selenium - Higher selenium levels are associated with reduced insulin resistance. In fact, supplementing with this trace mineral has improved my own and my insulin resistant patients' glucose levels. (Typical daily dose: 200–400 mcg.)

Cinnamon - In the past five years, solid research, first in India and now elsewhere, has demonstrated the value of the ground-up bark of the cinnamon tree in dramatically lowering glucose levels of diabetics and insulin-resistant individuals. The spice acts just like insulin on insulin receptors, allowing cells to take up sugar. (Typical daily dose: Start with 500–1,000 mg (¼–½ teaspoon) twice a day.)

Chromium - The trace mineral chromium interacts with insulin receptors and improves insulin's action. Moreover, research has shown that rats on chromium-deficient diets die young, while rats given chromium supplements have longer

Chapter 3: The Diet at a Glance

than normal lifespans. (Typical daily dose: 400–1,000 mcg of chromium picolinate or GTF chromium.)

You should also increase your spice intake as these are known to increase weight loss. Spicy foods raise the metabolic rate and speed up weight loss. In addition to that, you can use salad dressing, but choose the unprepared ones. Extra virgin olive oil is a rich dressing.

Condiments are also okay, but make sure they are not made with natural or artificial sweeteners as are ketchup, barbecue sauce, mustard, salsa, hot sauce, soy sauce, tomato sauce, vinegar, or Worcestershire sauce. Apple cider vinegar is preferred. Nuts and seeds are also good snack alternatives if they are raw and unsalted. Peanuts are good, but they should be roasted and unsalted and limited to ¼ cup twice a day.

It is very important that you consult a physician before undertaking any diet plan or health regimen. If you are also taking maintenance medicine for hypertension or blood sugar, your vital signs need to be monitored regularly. You may feel faint or dizzy during the first few times. You should also undergo the tests below prior to starting the Diet Evolution:

- Blood pressure
- Heart rate
- Fasting glucose level
- Hemoglobin A1C
- Fasting insulin level

- Fasting lipid panel (preferably with fractions of LDL and HDL, Lipoprotein(a) or Lp(a), Apo B, Lipo-PLA2)

- Homocysteine

- Fibrinogen

- C-reactive protein (CRP)

There are three important phases that you will go through in the Diet Evolution plan. The first phase is the "You Don't Have to Store Fat for Winter" phase wherein you'll concentrate on protein foods and lose weight. The second phase is the "You're Not a Threat to Future Generations" phase. In this stage, you will increase your protein intake through vegetables to trick your genes. The "Your Staying Alive Ensures Your Genes' Future" phase focuses on longevity through calorie optimization.

The three phases are to ensure that you take it step-by-step and not engage in a crash diet. Crash or fad diets always fail because they are not planned strategically. In Diet Evolution, your body adjusts to the changes gradually. In fact, you will hardly notice that 90 days have passed since you started the first two stages. In three months, your body replaces 90% of its existing cells. A continuous diet will transform you into a totally new cell system.

In this diet, you also have to adjust your lifestyle or movements according to your diet. Therefore, you may need to perform cardio exercises and copy what animals normally do. Supplements are also recommended because not all plant nutrients are readily available.

Chapter 3: The Diet at a Glance

You will also learn about the story of a supposedly "healthy" doctor who was slim, jogged regularly, and ate the proper food but still had hypertension and diabetes. His "killer genes" were activated because he was exerting too much energy in obtaining a lesser quality of foods. In the long run, the doctor followed the Diet Evolution program and really became physically fit, and his blood sugar, triglycerides, and HDL all normalized.

Chapter 4:
The First Two Weeks

This first stage is much like peeling old paint off a house before applying a new coat. You'll eat a lot of vegetables and get your calories from approved protein. Avoid deep-frying or cooking your foods too much, and if you're going to use some oil on your veggies, use olive or canola. The problem with most diets is that they skip this foundational stage. This is the stage at which you turn around the messages you've been feeding your genes, letting them know there's no need to store fat. Bottom line is, if you ignore this phase, you'll find it difficult to sustain any diet changes you make later on. It's like you getting the soil ready for planting. You get to do it only for some time, before work starts.

The vegetables and proteins you'll eat in these two weeks will be in proportion of More to Less, meaning you'll eat more of vegetables and very little protein, preferably not more than the size of your palm. Remember that the best vegetables are the leafy, green ones. You also get to snack minimally on nuts and seeds. If you're not cool with the animal protein, you could substitute with any of the following:

- Cottage cheese
- Swiss cheese
- Almond milk (plain)

- Yoghurt (plain and unsweetened)
- Free-range eggs
- Tofu

Eating animal protein at this stage is reminiscent of your ancestors who ate a lot of animal protein during winter, when there were no plants and they had to survive. In other words, you're tricking your genes into believing it is dry season and you need to burn fat, not store it. Another upside to the protein inclusion at this stage is that proteins require a lot of energy to be digested by your body.

In other words, you lose a lot of calories producing heat when your body tries to absorb protein. Lost calories equals weight loss, so, there you have it! But that's not all, the heat production itself stimulates a feeling of fullness, ultimately helping you to eat less and not aggravate your genes.

Remember we started this phase with a Vegetable-Protein combination. You know now what the protein helps you with. Vegetables, on the other hand, provide you with much needed nutrients, the kinds your ancestors fed on so long ago. Because vegetables are such a darling, you can eat as much as you want; you don't have to stop till you're full. Just make sure you're eating the right ones. The leafier they are, the better. The greener they are, the better. Eat a lot as raw salads and resist the urge to cook, except if absolutely necessary. Best part, you can eat it anytime- breakfast, lunch, or dinner, or even every time. And if that is not so good news for you, no biggie. Just take your time and gradually increase your intake portions. You really need the veggies, a variety of them. There

Chapter 4: The First Two Weeks

are more than one leafy greens you can find, and even some that are not so leafy but do your body good all the same.

Eating your vegetables will work maximally if you also include snacks of seeds and nuts, or both. Drinking 8-10 glasses of water also helps. You may even spice things up with some red wine or pure spirits.

Another thing to note during this stage is that eating foods- animal or plant- high in protein is not the same as eating food high in fats. Protein helps you shed calories while fat has not been proven beneficial.

So far, you have read that you can snack on seeds and nuts, but what exactly do they do for you? First off, the human brain will always seek glucose because that is its preferred source of energy, but because this stage allows zero carbs and sugar, that glucose is not readily available. But the brain is relentless. It goes raiding throughout your body for the glucose, and this raid could get it to strip other body parts of their nutrients. One of those parts is your muscle. Draining glucose from your muscle is one of the mechanisms through which a zero-sugar diet causes you to quickly lose weight, but it can also be harmful for your body, because you don't need our muscle collapsing. Nuts and seeds release protein and glucose in small quantities. That glucose satisfies your brain to an extent and keeps it from looking in and stripping the wrong places of useful nutrients.

Nuts and seeds also reduce hunger pangs, ultimately helping you to eat less. Just do well to stay away from salted nuts and seeds, or any processed stuff generally. It sort of defeats the entire process, doesn't it?

One of the pillars of this phase is a complete ban on sugar, but this is also maybe one of the most difficult things to achieve. You already know how our brains are wired to seek out sugar, salt, and fat. Since you know the enemy and the power it wields, and how your body is also a traitor in the mix, you should know how much work you have cut out for you. Fortunately, you can augment your efforts by taking supplements that have been proven to reduce sugar cravings. Selenium, Chromium, and Cinnamon spice are three of such effective supplements.

Another necessary component of this stage is the replenishing of bacteria in your body. Don't get scared. It's the right kind of bacteria, such as L. rhamnosus and Bifidobacterium bifidum that you need. You need the benefits derived from these bacteria, especially if you've been taking antibiotics and eating the wrong kinds of food. You can find supplements containing these helpful bacteria and use them.

But they need to be used alongside what is called prebiotics. The best form of prebiotics are Fructo-OligoSaacharides, but you can just call them FOS. They help you perform three functions:

- Reducing your cholesterol level
- Taking in more calcium and magnesium
- Boosting your immune system

You'll find FOS in onions, bacon, artichokes, garlic, etc.

Chapter 5:
What's Off the Menu?

Since Phase 1 requires you to stay away from sugary and high-carb foods, remember to avoid "Unfriendly Foods." You also need to stay away from your "normal foods" such as berries, brown foods like chocolates, fruit-vegetables like tomatoes, and cooked root crops.

In this teardown phase, you need to emphasize that the goal is to teach the body that "winter is here" yet you don't need to consume all those sugary foods and store fat. Yes, there are exceptions, but that doesn't mean that you have to stick to these exceptions. You have to change your lifestyle and eating habits.

The first two weeks also require you to eliminate fruit. Fruit motivates your body to store sugar so it is better to stay away from them. You also need to avoid milk. Milk contains an insulin-like growth hormone that makes the body grow. It is specially made for infants because they need to grow up.

Also, you need to take it slow and easy. One main reason that crash diets don't work is that they are too abrupt. They don't give time for the body to adjust to the new routines and food groups. You need to master how to take control of your body and eliminate those cravings. You need to take control of your genes and not the other way around.

Now, since you'll be missing out on many vitamins and nutrients, you need to take four recommended supplements.

First, you need to take Vitamin E, which is rich in antioxidants. Make sure you buy the mixed Vitamin E or d-alpha tocopherols because these are the real stuff. You need to maintain a required dosage of as high as 1,600–2,000 IU per day.

Second, Vitamin C helps in repairing the body systems and cells. Vitamin C repairs collagen breaks and boosts other micronutrients. Animals produce their own Vitamin C when stressed; humans do not. Therefore, when you are stressed, take Vitamin C. The recommended dosage is 500–1,000 mg twice a day.

Third, magnesium is beneficial for muscle contraction and nerve conduction. Never combine magnesium with calcium because you won't get the full effects. Cardiac specialists believe that magnesium deficiency actually contributes to hypertension. You need to consume at least 500–1,000 mg per day.

Fourth, take folic acid and other B vitamins. These vitamins are essential in reducing the buildup of homocysteine. This amino acid is the culprit for coronary artery disease, stroke, and Alzheimer's. Recommended dosages of folic acid are: 800–5,000 mcg; B vitamins: 50–100 mcg or mg. Keep in mind that more than 300–500 mg of vitamin B6 can lead to neurologic problems.

The best way to succeed in this first phase is to keep a food diary. Write down your food choices. Record your

Chapter 5: What's Off the Menu?

achievements, too. This will help you feel good about yourself and monitor your health at the same time.

Chapter 6:
The Teardown Continues

After the first two weeks of reprograming your genes and sending them the right message, you're probably already seeing results; losing weight and feeling better. With your next step, not only will you be making a few changes to your diet here and there, you will also be telling your genes- by the foods you eat- that their survival is tied to your continued existence. This will initiate a rebuilding process and get your genes to work for your well-being.

You can now introduce fruits, but only certain types. Cherries, berries, plums, and grapes are some of these fruits. Not only do they enhance long life, they also contain special antioxidants that boost brain functioning. Oranges, grapefruits, and apples also fall in this category. Just make sure not to overdo them and do not eat dried fruit. They are not the same.

The 'Brown' foods can also be introduced at this stage. Lentils, beans, and whole grains can be cooked and enjoyed, but only minimally (ideally, a half-cup serving). If you're very particular about weight loss however, your best bet is to stay away from them.

You should also reduce your protein intake in proportion to your vegetables. Eat more of vegetables and very little of protein. By this, you're toning down on calories and stocking up on micronutrients so richly found in vegetables.

When it comes to weight loss and optimum health, Glycemic Index and Glycemic Load are not as consequential as we've been made to believe. We certainly do not need to get paranoid over them as many diet fads claim. Fruits, brown, white, and beige foods are the main culprits to look out for in failure to lose weight or reduce cholesterol.

The fact that we have good and bad cholesterol- HDL and LDL- is common knowledge, but you probably are not aware that even those two categories carry sub-categories. For instance, only one of the five types of HDL actually purifies your arteries. Contrary to popular opinion that places all the blame at the feet of your genes, research has shown that the sugar and starches you consume are responsible for how high or low your cholesterol levels are, and the ratio of good to bad ones that you carry.

One particular type of cholesterol you do not want is lipoprotein (a), otherwise known as Lp (a). Basically, it increases the risk of premature coronary artery disease and is as deadly as can be. Research has shown however, that Diet Evolution, combined with two specific supplements is able to overpower the Lp (a)- producing gene. This is not before you find out if you carry the gene though, so get tested.

It is a known fact that your triglyceride levels shoot up as you increase intake of brown, beige, and white foods, as well as fruits like ripe bananas and mangoes. Increased triglyceride means increased LDL cholesterol and weight gain. Yes, it's

Chapter 6: The Teardown Continues

possible to eat high-calorie foods without gaining weight, but not at this level. The best you can do is stay away.

You've read about how grains revolutionized human diet when they were discovered. They were nothing short of a miracle at the time, but nowadays, they have turned the enemy and are pumping our blood full of sugar. A very good example is oats. Contrary to what the American Heart Association (AHA) and advert messages have told you, oats are nothing more than sugar foods. The only oats that are healthy are the ones that were eaten by generations way before ours. They were called steel oats and are nothing like the processed ones we eat today. Same goes for corn and legumes, so even if you want to eat them, make sure they are in very little portions.

Fats and oils can be introduced at this stage, but the trick is to use the healthy ones; the ones that will not send the wrong messages to your genes. Once upon a time, fat was the enemy, but now we know that we need some fats, such as omega-3 fatty acids. These fats are naturally found in small fish like sardines, and big fish like swordfish.

Basically, it is found in fish that feed on sea plants- like algae. It is also found in fish that feed on the plant-eating small fish. That is the natural order. Unfortunately, most of the fish that get to us today did not feed on the right things. Other sources of this essential fat include:

- Olive oil (extra-virgin)
- Hemp seeds
- Walnut

- Avocado

Unlike these sources, oils gotten from grains- soybean, corn, etc. - are mainly concentrated with omega-6 fats. Although your body needs both fats, it needs them in balanced quantities because while omega-3 fats reduce inflammation, omega-6 fats increase it. Unfortunately, the bulk of our foods today are grain-based. Yes, the readily-available meat, fish, and poultry are those raised commercially and fed with grains. That is why you need to be intentional about eating vegetables and the right kinds of oil. Besides, if you're going to eat protein, make sure your fish is wild, your poultry (including eggs) free-range, and your meat pasture-fed. Another advantage of omega-3 fats, which is very key to your Diet Evolution objectives, is that it puts a leash on your sugar cravings.

As usual, there is also the role of supplements. The following are only some of the supplements that can be incorporated in this stage of your journey:

- Mushroom extracts
- Cranberry extract
- Pycnogenols
- Magnesium, which helps manage hypertension
- Olive leaf extract
- Fish oil supplements
- Hempseed oil

Chapter 6: The Teardown Continues

- Flaxseed oil

Try not to forget these three things:

- Your ancestors did not eat grain-based oils. It didn't even exist during their time!

- Avoid modified foods. The more modified, the unhealthier

- The longer a food's shelf-life, the shorter it makes your life span

Chapter 7: Settling In

After a few weeks, you'll be pleased with what you are seeing and feeling, proving how focused you are. You will be feeling more positive about everything in your life, and the glitches within your body are noticeably subsiding. You might experience some dizziness or headaches while taking your medicines because your body is going back to normal. Ask your doctor to lower the dosage.

There will be times where you will notice your weight loss slowing down, which is mainly because your body is settling in; slowing down, and taking a few breaks to improve performance. It is slowing down due to the vanishing fat cells and not because the diet isn't working anymore, though your metabolism is still the same.

Instead of worrying about it, spend some time stabilizing your weight. Add more vegetables and keep lessening the proteins. Eating small amounts of fruit and "brown" food is okay if you've reintroduced them, as long as your weight stays the same. Whenever you have a slip up at this stage, it is highly recommended to go back to Phase 1.

As a tip, continue with your routine if the first breakdown happens during the first four weeks of the Teardown phase. If it occurs around the fifth or sixth week, then you need to continue with the phase until you achieve weight loss. This approach teaches you what it takes to maintain a lower weight. Your current eating regimen helps stabilize your weight and feel comfortable around it.

Know what your next step should be. It is better to go slow rather than be too fast. The hunger-stimulating hormone will be popping every now and then to send signals on how much you need food, but you must resist the temptations. During the summer, limit your fruit intake and have some more sleep.

When you sleep more, these hormones become less active. Also, you can't overeat when you're asleep. By purposely oversleeping, your hormones are tricked into thinking it is winter and storing fat isn't necessary.

The main purpose of the Teardown phase is to shut down the genetic program that makes you need to store fat. Though this program will always be in your genes, your body will continue rebuilding itself with new cells, as long as you avoid the "beige" and "white" foods and continue ingesting "brown" food in moderation. It is easy to tell how much weight was lost or gained based on the triglyceride levels delivered to your liver.

Here are some helpful Gundryisms to help you settle in and adjust as you go through the Diet Evolution:

- If you "push" to lose weight from a plateau, your genes will push back.
- Enjoy periodic plateaus; all assaults on the summit are done in stages.
- Sleep more, weigh less.

Chapter 7: Settling In

- If your triglycerides are rising, "white" and "beige" foods or one of The Dirty Dozen are creeping back into your diet, and you'll start to store fat again.

- If you're fantasizing about food, your hunger hormone ghrelin is sky-high; add more greens and omega-3 fats, and it will drop.

- The mind-body connection is real: Get those feel-good hormones activated with exercise, yoga, or tai chi.

Chapter 8:
Begin the Restoration

The goal in this stage is to get you eating like our long-time ancestors, the ones who lived before the discovery and practice of agriculture. So far, the diet in the first stage got you eating foods similar to how our more recent descendants did. In their case, they lived relatively better lives than us, but it was nothing compared to the lives of our early ancestors, who ate predominantly plants. They enjoyed a calorie sparse diet and that is what you should aim at if you want sustained weight control and overall wellbeing.

Don't be deceived by the tag "low-calorie" which is basically the coinage of manufacturers to deceive buyers. It does not mean the same thing a "calorie-sparse". As a matter of fact, low-calorie refined grains usually contain an insane amount of sugar. Basically, foods that are considered calorie-dense are those with large amounts of calories in their small quantity. This is where leaves prove without any doubt to be the healthiest choice. For instance, the calories present in about eight bags of romaine can be found easily in one tiny cube of cheese!

Going the raw and green route will see you eating mostly raw, green, leafy vegetables and you'll be the better for it. One of the functions of the micronutrients you get from vegetables is that they curb hunger; you feel full faster and eat less. The more leafy greens you eat, the less calories and more micronutrients your feed your genes. Even with your meat, poultry, or fish, notice how the healthy ones are those that fed on greens?

Not only do greens deliver the least calories, they also satisfy your genes in a very important way. Your genes require so many of the plant phytochemicals to perform specific important functions. For instance, Vitamin C is needed by your genes to prevent and repair wrinkles. What this means is that your genes will always need these nutrients. The more you eat them, the more satisfied your genes are. If you refuse to eat them however, your genes will continue to seek them, meaning you'll continue to bite from food to food until you find them. Bottom-line, you'll be eating more.

It would interest you to know that the fiber found in leafy greens is what speeds up the rate at which food travels through your lower bowel, triggering the release of anti-hunger hormones that tell you to stop eating. Research has shown that if you can eat one bag of dark leafy greens every day, not only will you be taking in less calories, you will also be making it clear to your genes that you are not a threat to the future generations.

At this stage, you should also phase out all the existing sources of calories in your diet- cheese, meat, and legumes. They served their purpose well enough in the first phase, but at this stage, the lesser you eat of them, the healthier for you. In the first phase, animal protein was a must-have, because you needed the high rate of metabolism and heat production it triggers to lose weight rapidly. But that was then, and unless you want your genes to pick up the signal that you're

Chapter 8: Begin the Restoration

struggling, that metabolism rate is not one you want to keep up.

As you might have figured out already, this phase is about you evolving your diet- eating more calorie-sparse foods, greener, leafy vegetables; reducing animal protein, legumes, and grains. You should stay in this phase for at least six weeks. Your protein will begin to come mostly from vegetables, eggs and nuts. Plus, there are innumerable nutrients and phytochemicals from which you can benefit when you eat vegetables. Continue to avoid the foods classified as white or beige, and if you must legumes or whole grains, reduce it to the barest minimum. You can continue snacking on nuts and seeds in this stage.

Finally, reorient yourself to think of animal protein as side dish, lesser in size to your main dish, which should be a bouquet of green leaves.

Chapter 9:
Picking up the Pace

In this chapter, you will be introduced to a fitness routine. Dieting does not necessarily need to be accompanied by going to the gym. What you need to do is to copy your ancestors' actions when they went out to obtain food.

One of the things that you need to remember in Diet Evolution is that you need to develop a habit. If you do something every day at the same time and the same way, you get used to it.

You'll suddenly realize that when you are unable to perform your habit, you feel that something is missing. For example, if you are used to doing your stretches as soon as you wake up, you'll feel sluggish if you are in a rush and do not have time for your morning stretches. With that, here is another Gundryism to keep in mind, "To earn it, you must burn it."

One of the activities that you need to do is take a walk. Animals and our ancestors moved because they needed to find food or keep their food from being stolen. It is recommended that either you do slow and steady for long distances or fast and abrupt for short distances.

Observe some runners in a marathon. You will notice that they are pale and have a sickly pallor as compared to sprinters. Marathon runners' immune systems go down because they need to run fast for a long period of time. Remember that expending too much energy activates those killer genes.

If you must run, go short distances and make it abrupt. If you want to walk, go long distances and go slow and steady. Just like our ancestors, who needed to sprint to the nearest tree or cave to escape a predator. Which leads us to another Gundryism – "If you run sprints fast, you'll gain muscle mass."

Heavy lifting or strength training is beneficial just like your ancestors. Heavy lifting gains muscle mass. You lift heavier things but with fewer repetitions or reps. Therefore, you don't use too much energy for a more extended period of time. Rather, it contributes to an adrenalin rush instead of feeling tired.

One tip is that whenever you go to the supermarket, use two baskets instead of a grocery cart. This method ensures that you perform some heavy-duty lifting and squatting. You hit two birds with one stone – you get your grocery shopping done and do some exercises. This also prevents you from compulsive buying.

You also need to reduce your insulin levels. Insulin is the culprit that tells your body that you need to store food and fatten up. When you gain muscle, your body screams for more food. Therefore, keep it slow and steady on the activity. Don't tire yourself and create more insulin in your body.

You also need to take muscle supplement that aid in muscle mass production. Among the recommendations is Coenzyme Q-10 or CoQ10, which is for muscle strength and stamina. The recommended dose is at least 50 mg; to reduce Lp(a) levels, at

Chapter 9: Picking up the Pace

least 150–250 mg is useful. Acetyl-L-carnitine or L-carnitine transports the energy into the muscle cells. Recommended dosages are 125–250 mg of acetyl-L-carnitine or 250–500 mg of L-carnitine, twice a day.

Here is another set of Gundryisms for you to memorize as you go through the Restoration phase:

- If you cut down on meat, you'll reduce your heat.

- A lot of greens plus a bit of meat make a meal that can't be beat.

- If you eat dark green, you'll become lean.

- The more you eat greens, the better you'll fit into your killer jeans!

- To earn it, you must burn it.

- If you lift weights, you'll lose weight.

- If you run long, go slow; if you run short, go fast.

- Sprint fast, and you'll build muscle mass.

Chapter 10:
Thriving for a Good, Long Time

This final phase concentrates on getting you beyond the "weight loss" thinking to the "thriving life" mentality. As such, you will need to go back even farther in time, when your earliest ancestors did not know about cooking and ate their vegetables raw. As unpalatable as that may sound to you, it is an established fact that raw plants contain the highest concentration of nutrients and phytochemicals. They also help you consume lesser calories because they're bulkier. The amount of nuts and seeds snacks you eat must also be halved at this stage.

When our human body systems come in contact with low levels of poisonous and unfavorable substances not enough to harm us, we produce a response known as Hormesis. Interestingly, Hormesis makes a person more resistant to survival threats. When the unfavorable condition is aggravated though, killer genes are activated.

Eating lesser calories produces another instance of hormesis, and has been repeatedly proven by research to elongate life span. This is why mainly vegetables tend to be shorter but live longer. To deal with plant toxins, their genes initiate a process that inhibits them from growing and reproducing rapidly, thus living longer. Vegetables with a bitter taste are the ones that trigger this process the best. So, when choosing your vegetables, although you may not jump at it, remember bitter is better.

This new diet of yours will be enhanced by a couple of practices you should embrace. They'll also help you initiate hormesis, and ultimately, a longer, thriving life.

Cook less and less of your vegetables. Hormesis is induced by plant toxins, and you'll lose most of that with cooking. Like most new stuff, it will likely be challenging trying to switch to raw vegetables, so take your time to ease into it. You can even start by cooking your vegetables halfway to gradually get your taste buds used to raw veggies. You might also experience side effects from eating raw veggies, so you don't want to overdo it the first time. As you read earlier, slow and steady is the best.

Explore bitter vegetables if you want to unlock your longevity genes. Kale, collards, red and green cabbages, are some of the less popular vegetables. Sad, because they pack the most nutritional value. Try them. And you don't even have to eat them alone. You can spice things up with some lemon juice and olive oil. Yum!

Eat the 'weird' vegetables. Algae, Nori, and Seaweed are but a few of these uncommon but highly nutritious plants.

Eating only raw foods works wonders for your body, but not everyone can do it. Do not beat yourself if you find it hard to give 100% compliance. Do what you can at the moment, and continue to push your boundaries- at your own pace- to see just how farther you can go.

Chapter 11:
Tricking Your Genes: Beyond Diet

Fasting is the best way to trigger hormesis. You can fast by drinking only water, coffee, diluted lemon juice, or vegetable juices. It simply means consuming less than you normally do. After a days' fasting, you can eat for two days' worth. You can also skip a meal or two and eat everything at dinnertime.

Another alternative technique is consuming a glass of wine every day. Wine and spirits, in low doses, stimulate the blood vessels. When this happens, they manufacture tissue plasminogen activator or tPA, which is used to dissolve clots after a heart attack or stroke. Alcohol also stimulates the blood vessels to produce nitric oxide that prevents blood vessel constriction.

The red grapes used in wine produce resveratrol (a phytochemical) that activates anti-aging genes. Also, the higher the elevation where the grapes are produced means that resveratrol is higher. Therefore, wine produced in Sardinia is the best source of resveratrol. This brings us to another Gundryism: "if you drink red wine, you'll be fine!"

Dark chocolate is from cocoa plants. EGCG, a phytochemical in cocoa, also has a beneficial effect. You can use 70% dark chocolate to nibble on or use in smoothies with vanilla-flavored soy milk. Black and green tea and coffee also have phytochemicals and promote longevity and good health.

Furthermore, expose yourself to a higher than normal temperature in a short period of time. This activates the heat-shock proteins that make the cells resistant to damage. A brief period in a sauna, steam room, or hot springs, as well as exposure to extreme cold in short periods, activates the longevity genes. When it is extremely cold, it compares to hibernation and hormesis is activated, too.

Exercise or movement and strength training are crucial to building muscle mass. Also, if you feel you need to rest, you can have one cheat day and eat pizza, but you have to compensate for it the next day by fasting. Vitamins are also beneficial and unhealthy. Stick to low doses of things such as antioxidants. Otherwise, high levels will work against your body.

You have to successfully build your routine and be in control of your cravings and should stick to it. This is another reason why diets fail. Because people tend to cheat regularly, especially when their insulin levels are high, and the carbs go directly to the problem areas. You can rest, but don't overdo it. Otherwise, you'll break your habit and must start all over again. If you've come this far, be proud and stick with it.

And now, here are another set of Gundryisms to memorize for a healthier, longer life:

- If you eat less, you'll live longer.
- Eat food "live" to arrive at a hundred and five.

Chapter 11: Tricking Your Genes: Beyond Diet

- Vegetables are good for you because they're "bad" for you.

- Exercise is good for you because it's "bad" for you.

- Drink some red wine, and you'll be fine.

- Keep your genes guessing as to the timing of your next meal.

- The cooler your engine runs, the longer you'll go without a major breakdown.

Quiz and Answers

1. Your genes are concerned about preservation, for themselves. How many directions are stated in this book

    a) 2

    b) 4

    c) 3

2. Having a large waistline is one of the signals that the killer genes have been activated.

    a) No

    b) Yes

    c) Not sure

3. At the same time, if you live in a place where meat is abundant, why would you settle for hard-to-obtain veggies?

    a) Veggies is also known to keep our body warmer, so when the climate changes, the diet also evolves. Man's diet evolves due to what is abundant now. Again, survival is the goal.

b) Meat is also known to keep our body warmer, so when the climate changes, the diet also evolves. Man's diet evolves due to what is abundant now. Again, survival is the goal.

c) Not sure

4. How many phases are there when going through the Diet Evolution plan

   a) 4

   b) 3

   c) 2

5. Which one is not a helpful Gundryisms to help you settle in and adjust as you go through the Diet Evolution

   a) If you "push" to lose weight from a plateau, your genes will push back.

   b) Enjoy periodic plateaus; all assaults on the summit are done in stages.

   c) Don't Sleep more, Don't weigh less.

Chapter 11: Tricking Your Genes: Beyond Diet

Answers

1. C
2. B
3. B
4. B
5. C

Conclusion

In the Diet Evolution, you are presented with a different way of approaching your eating habits. The goal is to go through the different phases in a given set of time. You will trick your genes into working for you and controlling them. You will learn to deal with food cravings because these are your genes telling you to fatten up or else.

The body develops because it is controlled by genes acting on autopilot. The genes tell the body what to do. You need to take control of these genes and not let them control you. Your cravings and eating habits also tell you that genes are controlling you.

You are also introduced to the concept of "killer genes" that control your eating habits and your cravings. They are the ones responsible for enticing you to eat unhealthy foods without knowing it. These killer genes are also responsible for propagating life and transferring traits to your offspring. Killer genes make sure that "they" survive and not the host.

The "killer genes" are activated they feel that you are exerting too much effort for low-quality foods. Or maybe because you are a threat to food consumption because you are already getting fat, so you need to be eliminated through diseases. Much as it is surprising, you are presented with factual data based on intensive research and studies with years of experience.

You also read about experiences with patients and friends who have suffered from obesity, diabetes, hypertension, and many other health conditions. Most of them already spent a couple hundred dollars for treatments, medication, and even surgery that did not help at all. In fact, being an obese heart surgeon led to the initiative of establishing the Diet.

Thank You and more...

Thank you for taking the time to read this book, I hope now you hold a greater knowledge about **Dr. Gundry's Diet Evolution.**

If you know like-minded individuals like you who would like to learn about **Dr. Gundry's Diet Evolution,** this information can be useful for them as well. So, I would highly appreciate if you post a good review on Amazon Kindle after you have purchased and read this book. Don't forget to share it on your social media (Facebook, Instagram, etc.).

Not only does it help me make a living, but it helps others obtain this knowledge as well. So, I would highly appreciate it!

www.amazon.com

FURTHER READINGS

If you are interested in other book summaries, feel free to check out the summaries below.

1- Summary – Hillbilly Elegy by Instant-Summary

   https://www.amazon.com/dp/B076Q9VQN5/

2- Summary – Dark Money by Instant-Summary

   https://www.amazon.com/dp/1979452334/

3- Summary – The Gift of Imperfection

   https://www.amazon.com/dp/B0776RSTY9/

4- Summary - All the Light We Cannot See

   by Instant-Summary

   https://www.amazon.com//dp/B07653T57B/

5- Summary – The Obstacle is the Way

   by Instant-Summary

   https://www.amazon.com/dp/B075PFY8CP/

*For more book Summaries, visit:

https://www.amazon.com/s/ref=nb_sb_noss?url=search-alias=aps&field-keywords=instant-summary

Made in the USA
Lexington, KY
05 November 2018